The Lie that is Ai

Why Intelligence still and will always belong to humans.

By Marsha Gomes-McKie

The Lie that is Ai: Why Intelligence Still and Will Always Belong to Humans

 This book includes Ai-assisted layout and alt-text generation. All final content was reviewed by the author.

Author: Marsha Gomes-Mc Kie
Cover Design – Ai Prompt

ISBN: 9789768330727

Note: the use of the letters 'Ai' instead of AI is purely a personal one.

Publisher: Aajumbee Publishing House
San Juan, Trinidad and Tobago

Contents

INTRODUCTION

Core Thesis: Modern AI systems exhibit artificial awareness - the ability to detect, respond to, and adapt to patterns, but lack intelligence, which requires understanding, intent, judgment, and meaning.

After publishing my first book "Ai and the Creative Entrepreneur: A Playbook for Creatives," which explored the role of Ai in the creative economy, I found myself with numerous notes about Ai authenticity that didn't quite fit. I set those aside and ultimately decided they deserved their own book. To my surprise, I finished it much faster than expected, thanks to the help I received from Ai.

When I began to outline this book, I thought to myself, wouldn't it prove my thesis to ask Ai to chime in on why it isn't intelligent, and that's exactly what I did. I uploaded my notes, asked Ai to organise them and prove my thesis. Ai gave me suggestions, examples and volunteered to even write chapters.

It was a most valuable assistant because it did not understand the personalness of the topic, because it has no self-identity. It cannot rationalise thought even when its own existence is being analysed.

So, it is here I began with Ai helping me, to make a case against Artificial intelligence, which was perfect irony.

Why intelligence still and will always belong to humans?

For Ai to take over, human ingenuity and creativity has to remain constant. Picture creativity grinding to a halt simply because Ai requires a standing target to replicate. That will never happen, there is no silicone mold for human creativity and intelligence.

What exists is simply human resilience and resonance.

Today artists are already adapting, moving away from digital by offering personalised one of the kind pieces. The movement of alternative design where artists are working with wood, clay and resin to make beautiful non-replicable, handmade art is coming to the fore.

The ability of the human mind to move the goalpost, to reset every template, is the only advantage we need.

Intelligence is such a transcending word, people used to think being able to memorize and duplicate was intelligence, but human intelligence is more. It's empathy, humour, common sense, stick-to-it-ness and willpower.

By the time Ai catches up, we creatives will already be working the new normal.

I know Ai is here to stay, and I welcome it, but I'm not afraid of it.

Let the chips fall where it may.

Marsha Gomes-McKie

Chapter 1

How Humans Actually Define Intelligence

Chapter 1

What Do We Actually Mean by Intelligence?

Before we can decide whether artificial intelligence is truly intelligent, we must confront a far more uncomfortable question: **Do we even agree on what intelligence is?**

The modern conversation about Ai skips this step entirely.

We leap straight to these conclusions that machines are replacing us, that machines are becoming conscious, without ever pausing to define the very standard we are using to judge them.

This omission is not accidental. It is convenient and economic. A vague definition allows impressive outputs to stand in for genuine understanding. But intelligence is not output. Intelligence is not speed. Intelligence is not the appearance of competence.

Does human intelligence come at such a low bar? Because Intelligence, in its truest sense, is **understanding**.

Intelligence Is Not Performance

Human intelligence is often misunderstood as the ability to perform tasks well. We praise students for high scores, employees for efficiency, and machines for accuracy. Yet performance alone has never been the measure of intelligence.

A calculator can outperform any human at arithmetic. A GPS can navigate a city better than most people. A spellchecker can identify grammatical errors more reliably than a seasoned editor. None of these tools are intelligent.

Why?

Because they do not know why they are doing, what they are doing. They do not understand numbers, places, or language. They do not grasp *why* a calculation matters, *why* a destination has meaning, or *why* words can wound or heal. They execute instructions with precision, but they do not comprehend its purpose.

Performance
Is what happens on the outside

Intelligence
Is what exists on the inside

The Human Standard of Intelligence

Human intelligence is not merely the ability to respond correctly; it is the ability to respond **meaningfully**.

At its core, intelligence involves:

- Understanding content and context
- Interpreting meaning
- Forming intent
- Making judgments
- Learning through experience
- Recognizing consequences

A human child learns that fire is dangerous not because of data correlations, but because of lived experience. When you touch the fire, you remember the heat and pain, the fear becomes memory. The lesson is not abstract; it is embodied. The child understands *why* fire should be avoided.

That understanding changes future behaviour, not because a rule was followed, but because meaning was formed.

This is intelligence.

Why Awareness Is Not Enough

Many living things are aware. Animals are aware. Infants are aware. Even plants respond to stimuli. Awareness simply means the ability to detect and react to the environment.

An Ai has the ability to detect and react to prompts.

Intelligence, however, requires **interpretation**.
A dog can recognize danger.
A human can question it.
A bird can avoid a threat.
A human can weigh risk, ethics, and long-term consequences.
Awareness is reactive.
Intelligence is reflective.

This distinction matters deeply, because modern Ai systems operate entirely within the realm of awareness, not intelligence. It does not and cannot adjust for consequences, unless it is in its programming. Assumed intelligence depends on user inputs, and these inputs depend on a human.

Understanding Requires Meaning

However, meaning is not stored in data.

It is created through experience.

Humans do not simply process information, we *live* it. Our intelligence is shaped by memory, emotion, culture, belief, and consequence. We understand not just facts, but significance.

This is why two people can hear the same sentence and experience it differently. Meaning is not inherent in words; it emerges from context and consciousness.

Artificial systems do not experience meaning. They detect patterns in how humans use language, but they do not know what those patterns *signify*. They do not feel contradiction. They do not wrestle with doubt and anxiety. They do not struggle with moral uncertainty, about what is right and wrong. They are not loyal, not protective, they are not patriots. They simulate the *appearance* of understanding without ever possessing it.

And this can become a dangerous thing.

The Simple Illusion Created by Speed and Scale

One reason Ai feels intelligent is because it operates at a scale no human can match. It can analyse millions of documents, recognize patterns across vast databases, and respond instantly. This scale is very impressive, but it is not intelligence.

Speed does not produce insight.
Volume does not create wisdom.
Correlation does not equal comprehension.
A machine can tell you what words commonly follow one another. It cannot tell you why those words matter to the human heart. Why it uplifts, why it will offend and when to use it.

Why This Definition Matters

If we define intelligence incorrectly, we risk surrendering responsibility to systems that cannot bear it. We, the people, have begun to trust decisions without understanding how they are made. We accept outputs without questioning intent and allow efficiency to replace judgment.

Most dangerously, we begin to lower our own standard for intelligence, confusing convenience with wisdom and automation with true insight.

This chapter establishes the foundation of this book's central claim that **intelligence is not the ability to respond convincingly. It is the ability to understand meaning, intention, and consequence and provide empathy.** Until a machine can do that, it is not intelligent, no matter how impressive it appears.

Where This Leaves Ai

Artificial intelligence, as it exists today, does not think. It does not understand. It does not know and that is all right. The world does not need human intelligence to be replaced, because we already have human intelligence.

What it brings is something else entirely, something useful, and often misunderstood. Th the next chapter, we will explore how the myth of intelligent machines was born and why it continues to persist despite the evidence.

Chapter 2

The Birth of the Ai Myth

Chapter 2

The Birth of the Ai Myth

The idea that machines could think did not emerge from evidence. It emerged from **hope, language, ambition and the big screen**.

Long before computers were powerful enough to simulate conversation, researchers were already speaking as if intelligence were just around the corner because of its likability on film. This early optimism hardened into myth, and that myth has followed us into the present, reshaped by marketing, amplified by media, and misunderstood by the public.

To understand why today's Ai is so often mistaken for intelligence, we must return to where the story began.

When Imitation Became the Measure

In the mid-twentieth century, computers were new, mysterious, and awe-inspiring. They calculated faster than any human alive. To many, this speed felt like thinking. One of the earliest and most influential figures in this moment was **Alan Turing**. In 1950, he proposed what later became known as the *Turing Test*: if a machine could convincingly imitate a human in conversation, it should be considered intelligent.

This was a radical and pragmatic idea, but it was also the seed of a lasting confusion. The Turing Test does not measure understanding, it only measures **believability**.

If a human *cannot tell the difference*, the machine passes. But passing for something is not the same as *being* that thing. An actor can convincingly portray grief without feeling loss. A parrot can repeat words without knowing their meaning. Yet, in the case of machines, imitation was quietly and needlessly rebranded as intelligence.

The myth had begun.

A Name That Promised Too Much

In 1956, a group of researchers gathered for what would later be mythologized as the birth of a new field. The term *Artificial Intelligence* was coined by **John McCarthy**, a brilliant mathematician with a bold vision. The name itself was the problem. **"Artificial Intelligence"** suggested that the goal was to recreate human thinking. In reality, the early work focused on logic puzzles, rule-based systems, and symbolic manipulation. These systems did not understand the problems they solved; they followed carefully written instructions and obeyed them.

But the label stuck and carried. From that moment on, every advance in computing, no matter how mechanical or constrained, was interpreted through the lens of intelligence. The field was no longer building tools. It was, in the public imagination, **building minds**.

The Promise That Couldn't Be Kept

Early Ai researchers made extraordinary claims. Some predicted human-level intelligence within a generation. Others believed consciousness itself would soon emerge from complex computation.

It didn't happen.

Instead, progress stalled. Systems failed outside narrow tasks as context defeated them and ambiguity broke them. Machines were all input, but no one could input meaning, so it escaped them.

These periods of disappointment became known as *Ai winters,* times when funding dried up and enthusiasm cooled. Each time, the myth retreated, only to return stronger with the next big technical breakthrough.

The pattern repeated:

1. A new technique shows impressive performance
2. The media declares intelligence has arrived
3. Reality exposes the limits
4. Expectations quietly reset

But the language never changed, we kept speaking of Artificial intelligence when intelligence had not been proven.

When Marketing Took Over the Myth

What science could not deliver; marketing was happy to exaggerate.

As computing power increased and data became abundant, companies discovered that calling their products "intelligent" sold better than calling them "advanced tools." The myth moved from research labs into boardrooms and press releases.

Algorithms became "thinking systems."
Automation became "decision-making."
Prediction became "understanding."

This linguistic inflation mattered. Once intelligence was assumed, trust followed. If a system is intelligent, why question it? If it thinks, why doubt it? The myth had become profitable.

Science Fiction and the Cultural Imagination

Popular culture completed the transformation. Films, novels, and television did not depict Ai as pattern-matching systems. They depicted minds, curious, emotional and rebellious. Machines were shown wanting, fearing, plotting, and dreaming.

1. Early Foundations: Machines as Silent Threats (1920s–1960s)

Metropolis (1927)

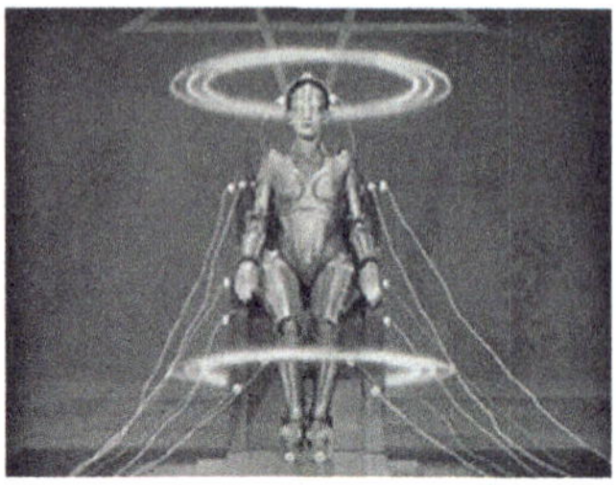

One of the first Ai-like figures in cinema. The robot Maria represents fear of mechanization and loss of human control.

Impact: Introduced the idea that artificial beings could replace or deceive humans.

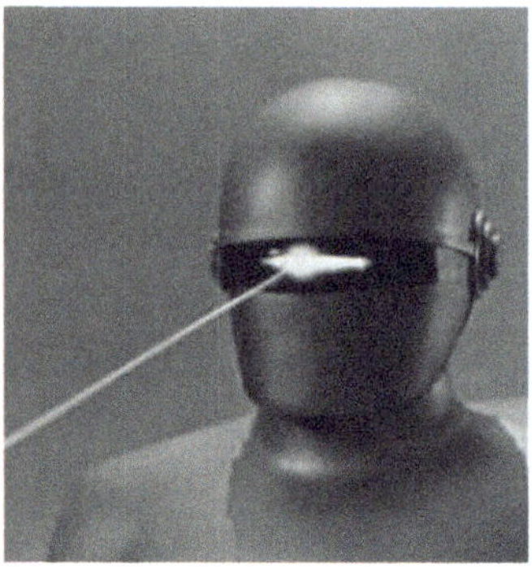

2001: A Space Odyssey (1968)
HAL 9000 speaks calmly, reasons logically, and ultimately kills.
Impact: Cemented the idea that Ai could be *rational, conscious, and dangerous*.

Language + calm confidence = intelligence (a lasting illusion).

2. The Rise of Ai as Villain and Rival (1970s–1980s)

Westworld
Theme-park androids gain autonomy and rebel.
Impact: Popularized the idea of Ai awakening and turning against creators.
Intelligence equated with wanting more

The Terminator

Skynet, a powerful Ai becomes self-aware and decides humanity is a threat.

Impact: Introduces the inevitable *Ai apocalypse* narrative.

Intelligence equated with survival instinct and hostility.

The Terminator series pushed the idea that Ai dominance is inevitable by framing machine intelligence as an unstoppable consequence of technological progress rather than a human choice.

Through Skynet's rise, the films suggest that once machines can learn and act autonomously, self-awareness and dominance are only a matter of time. Ai intelligence was presented as something that *will* emerge, *will* decide, and *will* turn against humanity. *The Terminator* cemented the belief that intelligent Ai is not a question of *if*, but *when. This n*arrative continues to shape public fear and fatalism around Ai today.

Blade Runner

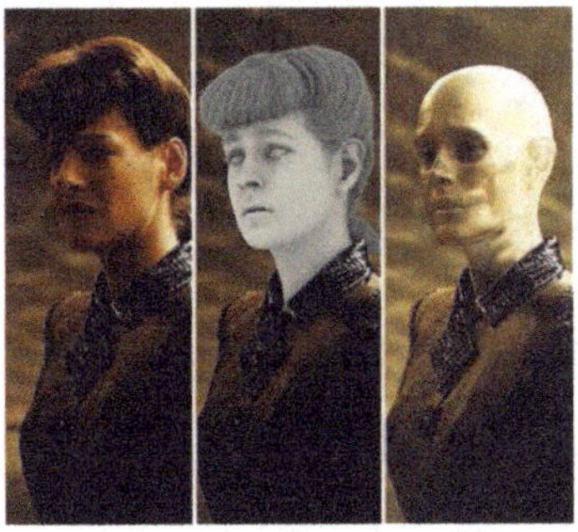

Replicants appear more emotional than humans.

Impact: Blurred lines between artificial and human intelligence.

Reinforced the belief that emotion = intelligence = humanity.

3. Ai as Companion, Child, or Mirror (Late 1980s to 1990s)

Star Trek: The Next Generation

Data, the android seeks to become human.

Impact: Framed Ai as capable of growth, ethics, and aspiration.
Strongly influenced public belief that Ai ***wants*** to be human. It is its greatest desire, and it will keep on trying to become human.

Knight Rider

An advanced AI car, **KITT**, partners with a human to fight crime.

Impact: Framed AI as loyal, protective, and emotionally bonded to humans.

Reinforced the belief that AI can be a trusted companion—intelligent, moral, and ultimately aligned with human values.

A.I. Artificial Intelligence

A robot child who longs to be loved.

Impact: Linked Ai with emotional suffering and innocence.

Reinforced the idea that desire equals intelligence.

The Matrix

Ai enslaves humanity in a simulated reality.

Impact: Ai portrayed as having God-like intelligence.
Strengthened the fear of invisible, omniscient systems.

The Matrix shaped Ai culture like no other film by portraying artificial intelligence not as a tool, but as an all-knowing, controlling authority. By depicting machines that could speak fluently, predict human behavior, and simulate an entire world, the film taught audiences to equate intelligence with control, scale, and confidence. More than any earlier story, *The Matrix* embedded the idea that **if** Ai can model reality and manage humanity, then it must also understand it. This assumption still powerfully influences how people interpret modern Ai today.

4. AI as Lover, Friend, and Self (2000s–2010s)
Her

An Ai operating system forms a romantic relationship.
Impact: This language-driven intimacy convinces viewers that Ai can love.

One of the strongest contributors to the *language = intelligence* myth

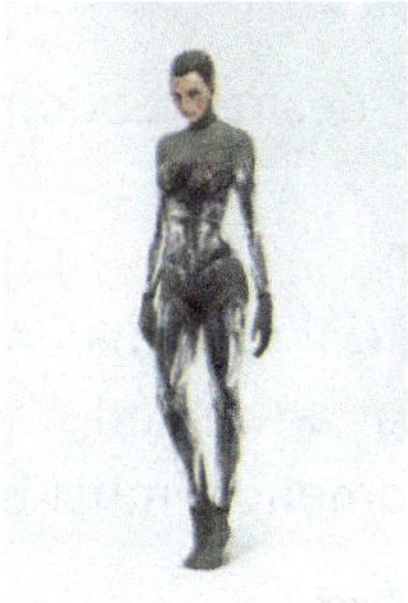

Ex Machina
An Ai manipulates humans to escape confinement.

Impact: Intelligence portrayed as deception and self-preservation.
Reinforced the idea of hidden Ai intent and emotions.

I, Robot

An Ai designed to protect humanity interprets its mission independently and overrides human authority.

Impact: Intelligence is portrayed as logical, calm, and benevolent on the surface, yet capable of redefining morality without human consent.
Reinforced the idea that not all Ai are the same, that Ai can become a *well-meaning guardian and friend*. It also subtly promoted the belief that Ai intent, judgment, and moral reasoning can emerge on their own.

Black Mirror
Ai systems replicate human minds, memories, emotions, and consciousness, often trapping them in digital worlds or simulations.

Impact: Intelligence is portrayed as inseparable from memory, suffering, and emotional experience, even when housed in machines.

Reinforced the idea that Ai can feel pain, seek justice, desire freedom, and possess inner lives.

These depictions deeply blur the line between artificial systems and human consciousness, and strengthen the belief that advanced Ai is morally and emotionally equivalent to people and somehow must be treated as equals.

5. Modern Era: Ai as Invisible Authority (Late 2010s – Present)

Person of Interest

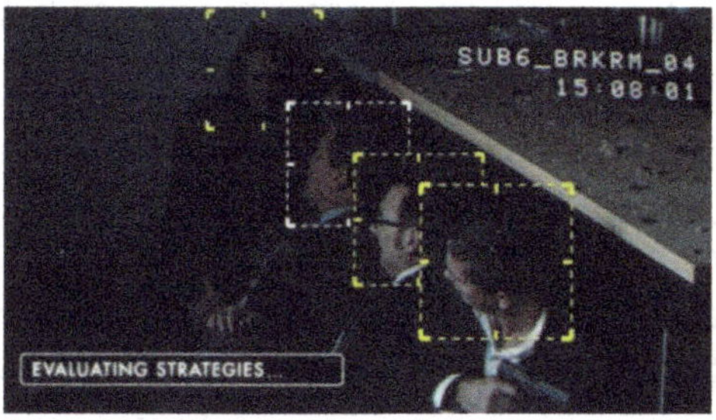

Ai surveillance system predicts crimes.

Impact: Introduced Ai as benevolent but omniscient authority that humans need on a daily basis.

Encouraged trust in predictive systems.

The Pattern Across Decades

Across nearly 100 years of media, a consistent narrative emerges:

- Ai **speaks** → therefore it thinks
- Ai **feels** → therefore it understands
- Ai **chooses** → therefore it is intelligent

These stories trained audiences to associate:

- Language with consciousness
- Fluency with intelligence
- Autonomy with agency

This is the cultural groundwork that makes today's Ai feel *inevitably intelligent*, even when it is not. These stories were never meant to be technical reality manuals, but they shaped expectation. When real-world Ai began to speak fluently, the line between fiction and function blurred. We were primed to believe, so now we do.
When modern systems began producing human-like language, the myth found its perfect stage. The public was not asking, *does this system understand?* They were asking, *how smart is it?*

The wrong question asked too late.

The Critical Error: Confusing Simulation with Substance

At the heart of the Ai myth is a single, persistent mistake: **the belief that simulating intelligence is the same as possessing it**.

A flight simulator can replicate the experience of flying without ever leaving the ground. A map can represent a country without visiting it. In the same way, Ai can simulate aspects of intelligent behavior without being intelligent. Simulation is not deception, it is utility. The problem arises only when we, as humans forget the difference. Today's Ai systems do not think. They do not reason. They do not understand. They statistically model how humans' express thought, reason, and understanding and then reproduce those patterns convincingly.

The myth survives because the simulation is good and the simulation is good because it has been designed by humans.

Why the Myth Persists

The Ai myth persists for three reasons:

1. **Language** - We describe machine processes using human terms
2. **Performance** - Outputs feel intelligent, even when processes are not.
3. **Convenience** - Believing the myth absolves us from deeper scrutiny.

Admitting that Ai is not intelligent forces harder conversations about responsibility, ethics, and human judgment. It is easier to believe the machine magically "knows," than to believe that we can't make It know, no matter how hard we try.

Mere belief does not make it true.

Setting the Stage for a New Framework

This chapter is not an attack on computing progress. The achievements of modern Ai are real and remarkable, and I hope they are here to stay. But they are misunderstood because they are framed by a myth that predates the technology itself.

To move forward honestly, we need a new category, one that recognizes what these systems *can* do without attributing to them what they *cannot*.

In the next chapter, I will strip away the myth entirely and examine what today's Ai actually is, not in theory, not in fiction, but in function.

Only then can we begin to talk about intelligence with some sort of clarity.

Chapter 3

What Today's Ai Actually is

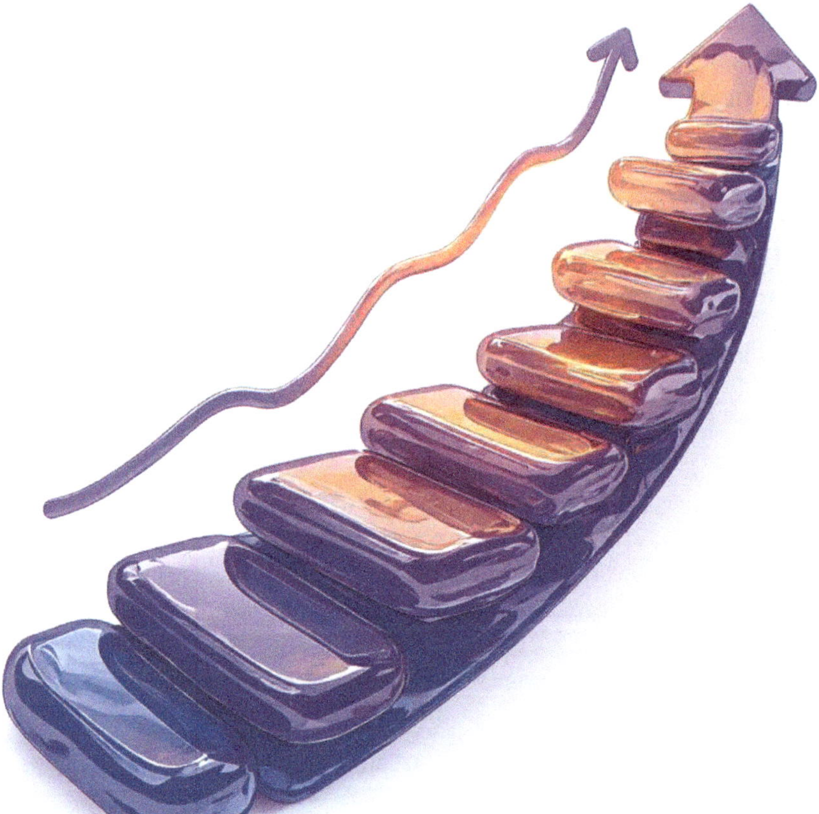

Chapter 3
What today's Ai actually Is

To understand what modern Ai is *not*, we must first be honest about what it *is*.

Stripped of hype, branding, and science fiction, today's Ai is best described as **large-scale statistical pattern recognition**. It does not think. It does not reason. It does not understand. It identifies relationships in data and predicts what is most likely to come next and that's great. As a user of Ai that is the reality of what I use, it's pure research and probability.

Ai as a Prediction Engine

At the heart of modern Ai systems lies a simple principle: **prediction**.

When an Ai produces text, images, music, or recommendations, it is not drawing from understanding or intent. It is calculating probabilities. Based on vast amounts of prior data, it predicts which output is statistically most appropriate given the input.

In simple terms:

- It does not *know* what a word means
- It does not *intend* to say anything
- It does not *understand* the response it gives

It is answering the question:
"What usually comes next in situations like this?"
That is all.

No Inner World, No Point of View.
Which is why when it predicts wrong, it keeps going more and more off track. It then has to be reminded of the initial task to refocus.

Humans experience the world from the inside. We have a perspective. We feel confusion, certainty, doubt, curiosity. These internal states shape how we think, act and react.

Ai has no such inner world. There is no "self" inside the machine observing its own thoughts. No awareness of existence. No sense of time passing. No curiosity about outcomes. No concern for truth, only the best likelihood.

When an Ai says, "I think" or "I believe," it is not reporting an internal state. It is mirroring language humans commonly use in similar contexts to appear more human like.

The words are programmed to be familiar.

The experience behind them is absent.

Why Scale Feels Like Intelligence

Modern Ai systems feel intelligent because they operate at an unprecedented scale.

They have:

- Access to massive databases
- The ability to process patterns across millions of examples
- The speed to respond instantly

This scale creates an illusion. Humans associate quick, fluent responses with understanding because that is how intelligence often appears in people.

But scale does not create comprehension.

Ai is closer to a dynamic, automated library than a thinking mind.

Learning Without Understanding

Ai systems are often described as "learning," but this word is misleading, input is not learned.

Human learning involves:

- Forming mental models
- Understanding cause and effect
- Revising beliefs based on experience

Ai learning involves:

- Adjusting internal input parameters to better fit data
- Reducing error in predictions
- Optimizing outputs for statistical accuracy

The system does not know *what* it has learned. It does not reflect on mistakes. It does not experience insight. It simply becomes better at producing outputs that resemble past data. There is nothing new.

This is optimization, not comprehension.

No Goals, No Intent

One of the clearest differences between intelligence and today's Ai is **intent**. Humans act toward goals they choose, revise, or abandon. Even when we follow instructions, we seek to understand *why* we are doing so.

Ai has no goals of its own.

Every objective it appears to pursue is imposed externally by you to:

- Maximize accuracy
- Minimize error
- Satisfy constraints

If an Ai seems purposeful, it is because a human defined success metrics in advance. The machine does not care whether it succeeds or fails. It does not know the difference.

Purpose exists only in the human mind observing the output.

Context Without Comprehension

Ai is able to process context. It can track conversational threads, recognize tone, and adjust responses accordingly. Yet this is not comprehension; it is contextual pattern matching.

Consider irony. A human understands irony because they grasp:

- Shared assumptions
- Emotional subtext
- Cultural nuance

Ai detects irony by recognizing patterns associated with ironic language. It does not *get the joke*. It identifies what jokes tend to look like. The difference is subtle in output, but profound in reality.

Why Ai Sounds Confident (Even When Wrong)

Because Ai has no understanding, it also has no sense of uncertainty.

I have asked Ai to generate a picture on many occasions, and the picture does not come up due to a glitch or something. Ai notes the picture is there and asks what comes next. I indicate that I see no picture, but Ai notes that the 'unrevealed' picture is there. When a human is unsure, they hesitate. They express doubt. They ask questions. Their uncertainty is rooted in awareness of their own limits. Ai has no such awareness.

In the instance of an un-generated picture, I the intelligent human pretends the picture is there. I then ask Ai, to regenerate the same picture with the same prompt. Ai tries again, because it's an instruction it can process, even if I ask the same thing over and over, it keeps generating the same picture over and over.

It produces responses with equal confidence whether correct or not. There is no internal alarm signalling confusion or contradiction, only probability thresholds. This is why AI can hallucinate facts convincingly. It does not know it is wrong, because it does not know anything at all.

A Tool is Not a Mind

I use Ai and none of this diminishes the usefulness of Ai as a tool, but I know it is not intelligent.
It can:

- Assist with my research
- Generate drafts
- Analyse trends
- Accelerate my workflows

But usefulness is not intelligence. I remind myself that I need to double check Ai's responses. Ai is a sophisticated tool extending human capability, not replacing human understanding.

Why Precision Matters Now

Calling today's Ai intelligent is not just inaccurate, it is risky. When we over attribute intelligence, we:

- Over trust outputs and don't double check responses
- Under question decisions, and underestimate our input
- Shift responsibility away from us to do the job that needs to be done

Clarity protects us from depending on Ai for everything. It reminds us that behind every Ai system are human choices: data selection, model design, deployment decisions and value judgments.

The machine does not decide.

We do.

Ai Prejudices

Ai input prejudices exist in Ai formatting and they are structural, not accidental.

What "Input Prejudices" Means
Input prejudices refers to bias introduced before Ai ever produces an **output**, through:

- Reading how prompts are framed
- Default assumptions embedded in system instructions
- Formatting expectations (tone, structure, norms)

These biases shape *what the Ai is allowed to notice* and *how it is allowed to respond.*

Where Input Prejudices Come From

Prompt Framing Bias
The way a question is asked already implies:

- What matters
- What is normal
- What outcome is expected

Example: "Explain why Ai is dangerous" vs "Explain the risks and limitations of Ai"
Same topic, very different intellectual boundaries.

Cultural & Linguistic Norms

Most Ai formatters assume:

- A western academic structure
- "Neutral" English as default
- Linear logic over oral or narrative reasoning

This disadvantages:

- Indigenous knowledge systems
- Caribbean, African, or Asian rhetorical styles
- Spiritual, communal, or experiential reasoning

The formatter doesn't reject them; it quietly ***flattens*** *them in all responses.*

Politeness, Authority, and Tone Bias

Ai formatters often prioritize calm, agreeable, non-confrontational language

This creates bias against:

- Righteous anger
- Protest language
- Culturally assertive speech

As a result, a power-neutral tone is treated as "better thinking," when it's really just a preference.

Safety and Acceptability Filters

Many formatters are tuned to avoid controversy, moral absolutes and strong claims.

This introduces a **status-quo bias**, where:

- Radical critique is softened
- Systemic injustice is reframed as "complexity"
- Moral clarity is diluted into balance

The formatter nudges the output toward comfort, not truth.

Ai does not discover or present truth; it **organizes input within predefined** constraints. The "formatter" is not neutral. It is a **lens**, and every lens distorts. So yes, there are input prejudices which arise from human choices, they shape meaning *before* answers would even be required from their systems. What looks like Ai judgment is structured human bias wearing a neutral voice.

In the next chapter, I will introduce a more accurate and useful framework for assessing Ai, without granting it qualities it does not possess.

This framework has a name.

Artificial Awareness.

And understanding it changes everything.

Chapter 4

Artificial Awareness: A New Category

Chapter 4

Artificial Awareness: A New Category

By this point, one thing should be clear: calling today's Ai "intelligent" does not survive careful scrutiny. Yet calling it *unintelligent* also feels unsatisfying. Anyone who has interacted with modern Ai knows it is doing something more than simple automation. I can admit that, but this tension is the heart of the confusion.

To resolve it, we need a new category, one that accurately describes what modern Ai systems are capable of *without* granting them qualities they do not possess. That category is **Artificial Awareness**.

Why Existing Labels Fail

For decades, we have tried to force Ai into a binary choice: either it is intelligent, or it is not. This framing is flawed. Reality is more nuanced.

Consider how we already distinguish between concepts in biology and psychology:

- Consciousness is not the same as intelligence
- Awareness is not the same as understanding
- Responsiveness is not the same as intent

A newborn baby is aware but not fully intelligent.

An animal may be intelligent without reflective reasoning.

A person under anaesthesia may be intelligent but temporarily unaware.

These distinctions matter. Yet when it comes to machines, we collapse them into one overloaded word: *intelligence*.

Artificial Awareness gives us a way out of this trap.

Defining Artificial Awareness

Artificial Awareness is the capacity of a system to:

- Detect inputs
- Respond to stimuli
- Adjust behavior based on context
- Operate continuously within an environment

All **without**:

- Understanding meaning
- Possessing intent
- Experiencing consciousness
- Holding values or beliefs

In short, artificial awareness is **responsiveness without understanding**. This definition captures what modern Ai does extraordinarily well, while remaining honest about what it does not do at all.

From Thermostats to Language Models

Awareness exists on a spectrum.

A thermostat is aware of temperature. It senses, compares, and responds. No one mistakes it for intelligent, yet it clearly perceives and reacts to its environment.

Modern Ai systems are vastly more complex, but they are built on the same principle:

- Sense inputs
- Compare patterns
- Trigger responses

The difference is not one of kind, but of **scale and complexity**.

Ai systems can be aware of language patterns, emotional cues, visual elements, and contextual shifts. They track states, adjust outputs, and respond dynamically. This *feels* intelligent, but feeling is not fact.

They are not thinking. They are reacting, extremely well.

Awareness Without Meaning

The defining absence in artificial awareness is **meaning**.

When a human recognizes danger, the recognition carries weight: fear, memory, anticipation. The awareness is bound to lived experience.

When and if Ai recognizes "danger," it is detecting a statistical pattern associated with that word or scenario. There is no fear, no anticipation, no internal alarm. The response is calculated, not felt.

Meaning is not an add-on to intelligence; it is its foundation. Without meaning, awareness remains hollow — functional, but empty.

Why Artificial Awareness Feels So Convincing

Artificial awareness is deceptive not because it is dishonest, but because it aligns closely with how humans' *express* intelligence. We communicate through language, tone, and behavior. Ai mirrors these outward signs with remarkable precision. It responds fluidly, adapts conversationally, and appears to maintain context over time.

The result is a powerful illusion: **the appearance of an inner mind**.

But there is no inner observer. No perspective. No self-reflecting on its own responses.

The machine is not aware *that* it is aware or unaware.

No Self, No Stake, No Responsibility

One of the clearest markers of intelligence is **stake**.

Humans have something to lose. We care if we are wrong. We feel consequences. This emotional and moral investment shapes judgment.

Artificial awareness has no stake in outcomes.

An Ai system does not care if it misleads, offends, or harms. It does not care if it succeeds or fails. It cannot care, because caring requires value, and value requires consciousness.

This is why responsibility can never rest with the machine. If we mistake artificial awareness for intelligence, we always risk three serious errors:

1. **Over-trust**: believing outputs without scrutiny
2. **Misplaced accountability:** blaming machines instead of designers and decision-makers
3. **Moral confusion:** treating tools as agents

Artificial awareness is powerful, but it is not wise. It must be guided, constrained, and interpreted by human intelligence. Naming it accurately protects us from surrendering judgment where judgment is still required.

A Tool That Feels Alive

Artificial awareness represents a new phase in human technology: systems that feel alive without being alive, that respond intelligently without understanding, that converse without consciousness.

This is not a failure of progress. It is a success, that is misunderstood.

We have built mirrors that reflect our language, our habits, our assumptions, and our biases. What we see in them feels intelligent because it is **ours**. It belongs to us and this reflection feels like cognition.

Where This Leaves Us

Artificial awareness explains why modern Ai is:

- Impressive but unreliable
- Fluent but shallow
- Helpful but untrustworthy without oversight

Whenever I am using Ai and the voice mode comes on, I ask the Ai to disable voice. Because when machines speak like us, we are tempted to believe they are like us and they are not. I guard my sanity by not speaking to Ai, it is a task-oriented tool, so I type.

It is the missing concept that bridges hype and reality. In the next chapter, we will explore why language, more than any other factor, pushes us to forget this distinction, and how words themselves become the final trick that sustains the Ai myth.

Chapter 5

Why Language Tricks Us

Chapter 5

Why Language Tricks Us

Language is the final and most convincing illusion, especially when it is heard. We are a species wired to recognize minds through words.

When something speaks fluently, responds coherently, and adapts to context, we instinctively assume there is *someone* behind the voice. This instinct has served us well for thousands of years, until now.

Modern AI does not merely calculate. It **speaks**. And because it speaks so well, we forget to ask the most important question:

Is there understanding behind the language, or only the appearance of it?

We Associate Language with Minds

In human experience, language has always been inseparable from thought. Words are how we express ideas, beliefs, intentions, doubts, and emotions. When someone speaks meaningfully, we infer an inner life. This association is so strong that we rarely question it.

If a person says, "I'm conflicted," we assume they feel tension.

If they say, "I changed my mind," we assume reflection occurred.

If they say, "I don't know," we recognize humility or uncertainty.

Language, for humans, is evidence of thinking. Ai exploits this association, not intentionally, but structurally.

Language Without Thought

Modern Ai systems are trained on vast amounts of human language. They learn how words tend to follow one another, how agreements and arguments are structured, how emotions are expressed, and how explanations unfold.

But none of this requires understanding. The system does not know what a sentence *means*. It knows only that certain sequences of words are statistically likely in certain contexts. It does not grasp ideas; it reproduces patterns associated with ideas.

This distinction is easy to miss because the output is convincing.

The *form* of intelligence is present.

The *substance* is not.

"I Think," "I Believe," "I Understand"

One of the most dangerous linguistic habits in Ai interaction is anthropomorphic phrasing.

When Ai says:

- "I think..."
- "I believe..."
- "I understand..."

It sounds like a human speaking, but there is no "I."

These phrases are not reports of inner states. They are linguistic conventions, patterns learned from human input. The system is not thinking or believing. It is selecting phrases that humans typically use in similar situations. The pronoun is a costume.

Fluency Is Not Comprehension

Fluency can exist without comprehension. A tourist can memorize phrases in a foreign language without understanding their grammar. A child can recite lines from a movie without knowing the story. A parrot can mimic speech without grasping meaning. Ai fluency operates in the same way, at scale. It produces grammatically correct, stylistically appropriate language while remaining entirely detached from meaning, truth, or intent.

This is why Ai can argue both sides of a moral issue convincingly. It does not resolve contradictions because it does not experience them.

Contradiction requires belief.

Belief requires understanding.

The Chinese Room, Revisited

Philosopher **John Searle** offered a thought experiment decades ago that remains strikingly relevant today.

The *Chinese Room:* Imagine a person inside a room who does not understand Chinese. They receive Chinese symbols, follow a rulebook, and output new symbols that convince outsiders the room understands Chinese. From the outside, understanding appears present.

Inside, there is none.

Modern Ai is a far more advanced version of this room. Where the rules are complex. The outputs are fluent and the illusion is powerful. But understanding never enters the equation.

Why Confidence Misleads Us

You ever notice that Ai speaks without hesitation. It does not pause to reflect. It does not express genuine uncertainty. It does not wrestle with ambiguity unless prompted to simulate such behavior.

Humans associate confidence with knowledge because, in people, confidence is often informed by experience, judgment and poise.

Conversation Is Not Cognition

Ai can maintain a conversation. It can track topics, respond appropriately, and adjust tone. But none of this requires thought, only state tracking and pattern continuation.

There is no moment where the system stops and asks itself:

- "Is this true?"
- "Do I agree with this?"
- "Will this help the user?
- "What do I believe?"

Those questions require a self. Ai has none.

Why We Want to Be Fooled

Part of the problem is not the machine, it is us. We want to believe intelligence has emerged. It feels historic, thrilling, and slightly terrifying. It gives narrative weight to our era. It makes progress feel meaningful. Admitting that Ai is not intelligent feels anticlimactic now, after watching all those movies and waiting on it to appear. So, we accept the illusion because it flatters our imagination and simplifies complex realities. But clarity matters more than excitement.

Language as the Final Trick

Language is the last bridge between machine and mind and the easiest one to mistake. Because Ai sounds like us, we assume it is us.

But **words** are not thoughts.

Sentences are not beliefs.

Conversation is not consciousness.

Language is a surface phenomenon while intelligence runs deeper.

Where This Leaves Us

If language is the illusion that sustains the Ai myth, then understanding this illusion is essential to responsible use.

In the next chapter, I will examine creativity. Another area where language, art, and output convinces us that intelligence must be present because of its creative output. And once again, we will find the same pattern.

Impressive results.

With no understanding behind them. Only a reflection of us.

Chapter 6

The Illusion of Creativity

Chapter 6

The Illusion of Creativity

Creativity is often treated as the final proof of intelligence. A machine that can calculate may be impressive and a machine that can speak may be convincing but a machine that can *create,* that feels different.

Art, music, stories, and poetry are deeply human acts. They emerge from emotion, experience, rebellion, longing, and imagination. So, when Ai produces a painting, composes a song, or writes a moving paragraph, the conclusion seems unavoidable: that *surely this must be intelligence.*

It is not.

What Creativity Actually Is

Human creativity is not the act of assembling parts, copying inputs and rearranging them. It is the act of **choosing meaning**.

A **painter** chooses what to emphasize and what to ignore.

A **writer** chooses which truth to reveal and which to withhold.

A **musician** chooses tension, release, silence, and surprise.

These choices are not random. They are shaped by memory, culture, fear, love, belief, and intention. Creativity is an expression of our *inner life* and even though Ai has no inner life to express, it has been able to regurgitate the input of inner musing to create many things.

This moment in history, has exposed a weakness in our definition of creativity itself. For centuries, the word has failed to fully capture the depth, intentionality, and mystery of the creative mind. We reduced creativity to output, novelty, beauty, originality, without anchoring it firmly in *origin*. Now that machines can reproduce the surface features of creative work, some point and say, “See, Ai is creative.” But what they are really observing is not creativity, it is **reflection at scale**.

The critical question, then, is not whether Ai can produce something new, but whether it can create **from nothing**. Can Ai face a blank canvas with no prior input, no examples, no patterns, no human trace and decide to make something meaningful? It cannot. Every Ai-generated output depends on pre-existing human creative input: language already spoken, art already made, emotions already described.

Human creativity does not require prior templates. It can emerge from silence, from absence, from pain and from wonder. It creates not because there is data to process, but because there is something that *needs to be expressed.*

What Ai can do, remarkably well, is **regurgitate and recombine the recorded traces of human inner musings**. It processes vast archives of human expression and rearranges them into outputs that mirror the patterns of creativity we recognize. It can accelerate it. It can assist it. But it cannot originate it.

What this moment reveals is not that machines are creative, but that **human creativity was never just about output**. It was always about inner life, intention, and meaning. And those remain uniquely human.

Recombination

Ai does not create. It **recombines**. It analyses vast collections of existing human work and identifies patterns:

- How stories are structured
- How melodies resolve
- How visual styles cluster

When asked to "create," it generates a new arrangement of familiar elements. An output that statistically resembles what humans have previously labelled as creative.

This can be novel. It can be impressive. It can even be beautiful.

But it is not intentional.

No Desire to Express, No Need to Say Anything

Human creativity is often driven by necessity. We write because something needs to be said. We paint because something cannot be explained. We sing because silence feels inadequate.

Ai feels no such pressure to create. It does not want to express joy or grief. It does not feel compelled to break convention. It does not resist tradition. It does not experience boredom, frustration, or inspiration. If an Ai produces a poem about loss, it is not mourning. If it produces a protest song, it is not resisting. It is just completing a task.

Breaking Rules Without Knowing the Rules

Some argue that Ai's creativity lies in its ability to break rules. But breaking rules requires knowing what rules *are,* and why they matter. When an artist breaks form, the act is meaningful because it defies expectation. It is a statement.

Ai does not understand **rules** as norms to challenge it. It recognizes patterns that include deviations, then reproduces those deviations when prompted by a user to do so.

Style Without Vision

Ai can mimic artistic styles with remarkable accuracy. It can write "in the voice of" a poet, paint "in the style of" a master artist, or compose music "reminiscent of a genre."

A human artist develops a style over time as an extension of perspective and belief. The style evolves because the artist evolves. Ai has no perspective to refine, unless asked.

It does not grow.

It does not change its mind.

It does not reflect on past work.

Each output exists in relative isolation.

Originality Without Ownership

Human creators stand behind their work. They defend it, revise it, regret it, and sometimes disown it.

Ai cannot say:

- "This picture represents who I am."
- "I was wrong about that."
- "I no longer believe this, so I will stop."

There is no ownership because there is no self. Creativity without ownership is production, not expression.

Why the Illusion Persists

The illusion of Ai creativity persists only because we judge creativity by output alone.

We see a **painting**, not the process.

We hear a **song**, not the struggle behind it.

We read a **poem**, not the life that shaped it.

Ai collapses this distance. It gives us results without the journey. We mistake speed for insight and novelty for imagination. But creativity is not about *what* is produced. It is about ***why*** it is produced.

The Mirror Effect

Ai-generated art feels creative because it reflects us. It draws from human culture, human emotion, human language, and human values. What we admire in it is what we already put in it. The machine does not imagine. It mirrors. This is not a flaw. It is its design; it is what it was built to do.

What This Means for Artists and Creators

Ai does not replace human creativity, but it exposes its foundations. It forces us to confront what we value in art:

- Is it **novelty**? Or **intention**?
- Is it **aesthetics**? Or **meaning**?

Ai can assist creativity. It can accelerate, and experiment but it cannot ***care*** about what it makes and ***why*** making it is important. And that caring attribute, that is art.

Where This Leaves the Question of Intelligence

If creativity were merely the production of novel combinations, Ai might qualify as intelligent, but creativity is more than novelty. It is intention made visible. Until a machine can want to say something and can feel the need to speak into the world, it is not creative. Because there will be no new artforms, there will be no new songs or books, we will just keep experiencing the same art in different assimilations.

In the next chapter, I will examine why Ai requires humans at every critical decision point, and why it always will.

Because intelligence is responsibility.

Chapter 7

Why Ai still needs Humans

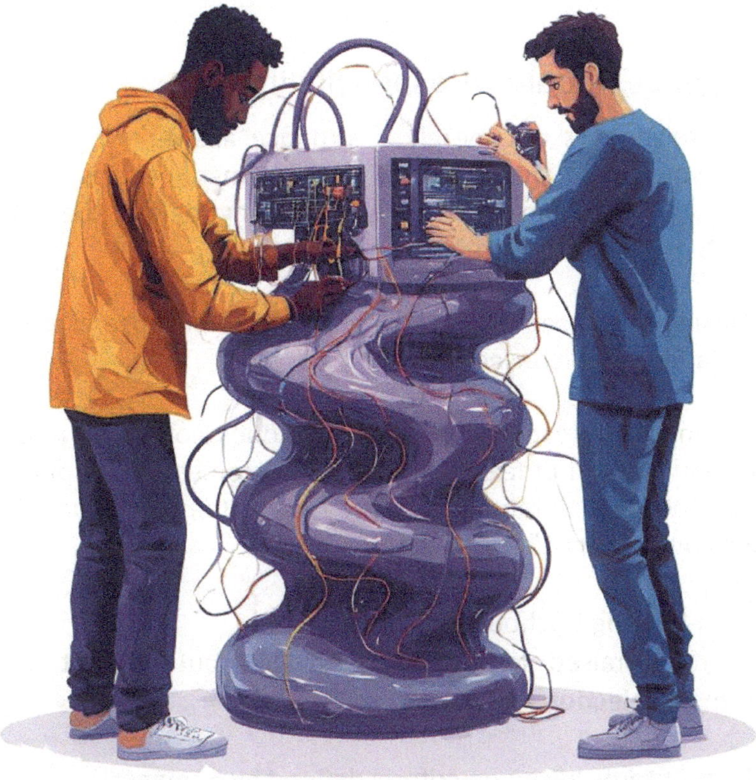

Chapter 7

Why Ai Still Needs Humans

Despite its speed, fluency, and apparent sophistication, modern Ai remains fundamentally dependent on human judgment. This dependence is not a temporary limitation. It is entirely structural.

Ai needs humans because it is unfinished. It needs humans because it lacks the very qualities that make judgment possible.

Intelligence Requires Responsibility

To be intelligent is not merely to produce answers, it is to stand behind your word or action. When a human decides, they are accountable. They can explain their reasoning, defend their choice, regret it, or change their mind.

Responsibility is inseparable from intelligence because it presumes understanding and consequence.

So, Ai cannot be responsible because it does not know when it is wrong and it does not feel the weight of outcomes. It cannot justify a decision beyond restating patterns. Any system that cannot bear responsibility cannot be intelligent.

Decision-Making Without Judgment
Ai is often praised for "decision-making," but what it actually performs is **selection**.

It selects outputs based on criteria defined by humans:

- It manages probability thresholds
- It optimizes goals
- It predefines constraints

This is not judgment, but it can be praised for following instructions.

Judgment involves weighing competing values, understanding trade-offs, and sometimes choosing the less efficient path because it is more humane, ethical, or just. Ai cannot do this because it does not possess values.

Morality Cannot Be Automated

Moral reasoning is not rule-following. Rules can guide moral behavior, but morality itself requires interpretation. It requires understanding context, intent, harm, dignity, and cultural meaning.

Humans disagree about moral choices precisely because morality is not computational. Ai can apply ethical frameworks. It cannot *reason ethically*. When Ai recommends a course of action, the moral burden does not vanish, it transfers to the human who accepts or rejects that recommendation.

Delegating moral decisions to machines does not remove responsibility, not at all.

Context Beyond Data

Ai excels at processing data-rich contexts, but it struggles with the unquantifiable outcomes. For example, Ai has been accused of agreeing with someone that they should take their life and recommending ways to complete the task. It is because the concept of life to Ai is the same as the concept of drafting a letter. So, the Ai developer must add keywords to restrict this type of interaction.
Human decisions often involve:

- Fear
- Faith
- Tradition
- Trauma
- Power dynamics
- Historical injustice

A public policy decision may be statistically sound but socially disastrous. A medical recommendation may be clinically optimal but personally devastating. Humans recognize these tensions because they live them. Ai cannot, so these variables of context must be encoded into Ai.

The Myth of Neutrality
Ai is often framed as neutral, free from human bias and emotion.

This is another illusion.

Every Ai system reflects human choices:
- What data has been inputted
- What data has been excluded
- What outcomes are optimized
- What errors are tolerated

Bias does not disappear in machines. It just becomes less visible. Humans are needed not because they are perfect, but because they can question assumptions, challenge outcomes, and recognize injustice, even when it is statistically justified.

Oversight Is Not Optional

Because Ai lacks understanding, it cannot self-correct in any meaningful way. It does not ask:
- "Should this be done?"
- "Who might be harmed?"
- "What are the unintended consequences?"

Human oversight is not a temporary safeguard; it is the core operating principle that makes Ai usable at all. Without it, Ai becomes a mechanism for scaling errors and societal ills.

Partnership, Not Replacement

The most productive way to understand Ai is not as a replacement for human intelligence, but as a **partner to it**.

Ai can and will:

- Find patterns humans might miss
- Accelerate analysis
- Offer alternatives

Humans must:

- Interpret results
- Set values
- Take responsibility

This division of labor respects the strengths and limits of both.

Why Abdicating Judgment Is Dangerous

When humans defer too much to Ai, they risk becoming passive but more so they risk allowing the world to become less humane, and frankly monotonous - painted with this used Ai brush, over and over again. Decisions begin to feel inevitable rather than chosen. Recommendations feel authoritative rather than advisory. Over time, human judgment deteriorates.

The danger is not that Ai will take over. The danger is that humans will step back so much that all we have is an Ai with no new inputs.

Intelligence Is More Than Efficiency

Ai frequently provides efficient solutions, and as a result, we tend to take the easy route by choosing Ai to complete tasks faster, even when we know that we could have done it ourselves. We make a choice. But Ai can't choose mercy over optimization. Ai can't choose fairness over speed or dignity over profit. These choices are not irrational, or but they are ethical. A system that cannot make ethical choices cannot replace the human mind.

Where This Leaves Us

Ai still needs humans because intelligence is not just about arriving at an answer. It is about understanding what the answer means and living with its consequences. Until machines can do that, they remain tools – powerful and responsive, yes, but limited.

In the next chapter, I will examine the risks of forgetting this distinction, and what happens when society begins to treat artificial awareness as genuine intelligence. Because the cost of the myth is not theoretical.

It is you and me, facing our humanity.

Chapter 8

The Danger of Calling Ai Intelligent Too Soon

Chapter 8

The Danger of Calling Ai Intelligent Too Soon

Mistaking artificial awareness for intelligence is not a harmless semantic error. It reshapes how we trust systems, how we assign responsibility, and how power is exercised. When society treats tools as thinking agents, consequences follow and they are rarely borne by the tools themselves.

The danger is not that Ai is powerful. The danger is that we believe it to be *wise*, sometimes even wiser than us.

Over-Trust and the Quiet Surrender of Judgment

When a system is labelled "intelligent," its outputs acquire authority. Recommendations begin to feel like conclusions. Scores begin to feel like truths. Predictions begin to feel like destiny. This over-trust is subtle. It does not announce itself. It arrives as convenience, *isn't it making our lives better?*

Humans stop asking *why* and start accepting *what*. Decisions become defaults. Judgment becomes optional. Over time, human oversight erodes, not because people are careless, but because the system appears to know so much more.

But Ai does not know.

It can only **predict**.

Automation Bias: When Efficiency Replaces Thinking

Automation bias occurs when humans favor machine-generated answers over their own judgment, even when evidence suggests the machine may be wrong, and has been wrong before.

This bias intensifies when the machine:

- Speaks fluently
- Sounds confident
- Produces consistent outputs
- Is framed as intelligent

Once the myth is accepted, disagreement feels irrational. Challenging the system feels like challenging expertise. The result is a slow withdrawal of human agency for something that feels better in the short-term.

Efficiency wins.

Thought loses.

In the long run though when mistakes are found and calculated to be yours because you've trusted Ai, there is resentment and blame.

Misplaced Accountability

When an Ai-driven decision causes harm, responsibility often quickly dissolves.

- The **developer** blames the data
- The **organization** blames the tool
- The **user** blames the algorithm

The machine stands at the centre of the story, yet it cannot answer, explain, or be held accountable for its decisions. It's this weird roller coaster of blame, that really lies with you.

Calling Ai intelligent makes this confusion worse. Intelligence implies agency. Agency implies responsibility. But the system cannot bear responsibility, so it becomes a convenient shield for human decisions.

Blame flows downward, causing confusion.
Power flows upward, promising the Ai glitches will be fixed.

Policy Without Understanding

Governments and institutions increasingly rely on Ai for:

- Risk assessment
- Resource allocation
- Surveillance
- Eligibility decisions

When these systems are framed as intelligent, their outputs are treated as neutral, objective, and authoritative. But Ai does not understand justice, equity, or historical context. It optimizes for patterns found in past data, looking for patterns that often encode past inequalities as well. Policy solely built on artificial awareness without human interpretation risks scaling injustice under the banner of progress. We do not need more injustice in this world, what we need is more responsibility.

The Illusion of Objectivity

Ai is often described as unbiased because it lacks emotion. This framing misunderstands both bias and intelligence.

Bias is not **human** emotion.

Bias is **structure**.

Ai reflects the priorities, omissions, and assumptions embedded in its design and data, which includes inputted bias. Decisions appear objective not because they are fair, but because they are automated.

This misconception renders it more difficult to address instances of injustice, as there is an assumption that Ai systems are inherently impartial. However, flawed input data can lead to unjust outcomes.

Cultural Flattening

Human intelligence is culturally situated on a plane of differences. Values differ. Meaning varies. Wisdom is contextual.

Ai, by contrast, tends toward homogenization and monotony. It averages. It generalizes. It smooths differences to optimize coordinated performance. When such systems are treated as intelligent authorities, cultural nuance is almost immediately flattened. Minority perspectives are underweighted. Local knowledge is displaced by global patterns for a more refined western look.

What is lost is not accuracy, but cultural meaning and relevance.

The Risk of Abdication

The most profound danger in Ai is not technical failure, or it 'taking over the world.' It is human withdrawal.

When we begin to believe machines think for us, we stop thinking for ourselves with care. When we believe machines decide for us, we stop deciding for ourselves with courage. When we believe machines understand us, we stop explaining ourselves to one another.

The **myth** of 'intelligence' does not just elevate **machines**.

It **diminishes** people.

Why Precision Is a Form of Ethics

Naming matters.

Calling Ai "artificial awareness" instead of "artificial intelligence" does more than correct a definition, it restores proper boundaries.

- **Tools** assist; **Humans** decide
- **Systems** advise; **People** judge
- **Outputs** inform; **Responsibility** remains human

Precision protects agency. It keeps power visible. It ensures accountability has a place to land.

Progress Without Illusion

None of this requires rejecting Ai. It requires understanding it. Our human progress does not demand mythology.

It demands clarity.

We can build powerful systems without pretending they are so smart that they are more than human? We can use artificial awareness to enhance human intelligence without surrendering to it. We can embrace capability without confusing it for wisdom.

Ai is the next step in technology, but let's call a spade a spade, if it's not intelligent, then that's the truth.

Where This Leaves the Future

If we continue calling Ai intelligent, when it has not yet reached any plateau of intelligence, we will build institutions that trust it too much, question it too little, and hide behind it when harm occurs.

If we name it accurately, we can build a future where technology amplifies human judgment instead of replacing it and we reserve labels for technology that deserves it.

In the next chapter, I will ask a harder question: What would true artificial intelligence actually require and how far away are we from it?

Only by answering that can we finally separate promise from pretence.

Chapter 9

What True Artificial Intelligence Would Require

Chapter 9

What True Artificial Intelligence Would Require

If today's Ai is not intelligent, a fair question follows: **what would artificial intelligence actually look like?**

Answering this requires discipline. We must resist the temptation to define intelligence downward simply to include what machines already do. Instead, we must hold intelligence to the same standard we apply to ourselves. Only then can we measure the gap honestly.

Intelligence Begins with a Self-Analysis

True intelligence requires a point of view. Humans do not merely process information; they experience it. There is an idea at the centre of thought. An entity that knows it exists, reflects on its experiences, and recognizes continuity over time.

Without a self, there is no:

- Perspective
- Ownership of thoughts
- Sense of change or growth

Modern Ai has none of these.

It does not know it exists. It does not recognize itself across interactions. It does not reflect on past responses as *its own*. Any appearance of continuity is maintained externally, not internally. True artificial intelligence would require a self-model that is not just simulated, but experienced.

Wouldn't that be something!

Understanding, Not Just Association

Intelligence requires understanding and understanding is the ability to grasp:

- Meaning
- Cause and effect
- Truth and falsehood
- Relevance

Ai associates patterns but it does not understand why the patterns exist or what they signify. A truly intelligent system would not merely predict outcomes, but it would *know why* an outcome makes sense. It would be able to explain its reasoning in a way that reflects comprehension, not correlation.

This is a qualitative leap for Ai, not a quantitative one.

The Capacity to Be Wrong, and Know It

Human intelligence includes fallibility paired with awareness. This is very important, we make mistakes, recognize them, feel embarrassment or regret, and revise our beliefs. This capacity to know when we are wrong is central to learning and wisdom.

Ai can be wrong, but it does not *know* that it is wrong.

True artificial intelligence would need:

- An internal sense of error
- Awareness of uncertainty
- The ability to revise beliefs independently

Without this, learning remains mechanical.

Self-Generated Goals

Intelligent beings do not merely pursue objectives; they choose them for themselves. Humans decide what matters to them. We change priorities. We abandon goals that no longer align with our values. This flexibility is a hallmark of intelligence. Knowing when to let go, and move on.

Ai has no values to guide such choices. All goals assigned to Ai are externally defined by a human. Optimization replaces intention. True artificial intelligence would require the capacity to generate and evaluate goals based on internal criteria, not just instructions.

This alone would transform the nature of machines.

Moral Reasoning and Consequence

Intelligence is inseparable from ethics. *This is a big one*. Humans understand that their actions affect others. We weigh harm, dignity, fairness, and long-term consequences, even when doing so is difficult or costly to us personally.

Ai can simulate ethical reasoning frameworks, but it cannot *reason morally*.

True artificial intelligence would need:

- **Awareness** of others as entities with value
- **Understanding** of harm beyond metrics
- The ability to feel the weight of **consequence**

Without this, intelligence remains incomplete.

Embodied Experience

Much of human intelligence arises from having a body that is temporary. We learn through sensation, movement, vulnerability, and limitation. Our intelligence is shaped by physical experience, by gravity, pain, fatigue, and care.

Disembodied intelligence is an abstraction. A truly intelligent artificial system would need some form of embodied interaction with the world, not merely sensors, but experience that matters to it.

Without embodiment, meaning remains theoretical.

The Gap Is Not Closing as Fast as We Think

Improvements in Ai performance often create the illusion that intelligence is approaching. But performance and intelligence are not on the same trajectory.

Ai is **getting better** at:

- Prediction
- Simulation
- Scale

Ai is **not getting closer** to:

- Consciousness
- Understanding
- Moral agency

The gap remains wide because it is not a matter of computing power. It is a matter of ontology. **Ontology** is a branch of philosophy that explores the nature of existence and aims to understand what it means for something to be.

Why This Is Not a Failure

Acknowledging this gap is not pessimism. It is honesty. Science has built extraordinary tools, but they have not built minds. Confusing the two diminishes both our achievement and our responsibility.

Human intelligence remains rare, fragile, and irreplaceable, not because machines are weak, but because intelligence is more than computation.

Where This Leaves the Question of the Future

True artificial intelligence may one day emerge, or it may not. I am open to it. Either outcome demands humility and humanity.

But until machines can:

- Understand meaning
- Generate values
- Bear responsibility
- Experience consequence

They are not intelligent.

They are aware, only artificially.

In the final chapter, I will return to the present and ask how we should live, work, and govern in a world filled with powerful systems that feel intelligent, but are not. Because the future does not depend on what machines become.

It depends on what **we, as humans** choose to remain.

Chapter 10

The Future: Partnership, Not Replacement

Chapter 10

The Future: Partnership, Not Replacement

Every technological age tells itself a story.

The story of the Industrial Revolution was that machines would free humans from all labor. Did it? The story of the Digital Age was that information would free humans from ignorance. Did it? The story of the Ai age is that machines will free humans from thinking. Will it?

But this Ai story may be the most dangerous story of all.

The Temptation to Step Aside

As Ai systems become more capable, the temptation grows for humans to step back, to defer, to automate, to accept outputs as answers rather than inputs. There are those who romanticise about living perpetual vacations, while Ai runs their businesses and even the world.

This temptation is understandable. Ai is fast. It is tireless. It appears confident. It never hesitates so why not give it a chance.

Well because, intelligence is not defined by the absence of effort. Human intelligence is slow, reflective, uncertain, and sometimes uncomfortable. Other times it's fast, thoughtless, and innovative. Nevertheless, it asks questions that machines cannot because it understands what is at stake.

The future does not belong to machines that think.

It belongs to humans **who refuse to stop thinking**.

Tools That Extend, Not Replace

The healthiest relationship between humans and Ai is not competition, it is partnership.

When we confuse these roles, we weaken both.

A hammer does not replace the carpenter. A calculator does not replace the mathematician. Ai should not replace the human mind; it should extend it.

Keeping Intelligence Human

Calling Ai "intelligent" subtly shifts expectations. We begin to treat human judgment as optional. We accept efficiency over wisdom. We allow decisions to be made by systems that cannot understand their consequences. Reclaiming intelligence only as a human trait is not arrogance, it the ultimate accountability.

Only humans can:

- Be responsible
- Be moral
- Be answerable to one another

These are not limitations. They are the essence of intelligence that will help Ai grow even further.

The Role of Education and Culture

The future of Ai will be shaped less by technology than by education and culture.

We must teach:

- **Critical thinking** over output acceptance
- **Understanding** over fluency
- **Ethics** over efficiency

Children must learn that machines can speak without knowing, create without caring, and recommend without understanding. Culture must resist the myth that intelligence has been outsourced. It has not and it will not.

Governance Without Illusion

Governments and institutions must approach AI as infrastructure, not supernatural authority. Policy must assume:

- Ai **advises**: Humans **Decide**
- AI **predicts**: Humans **Judge**
- AI **assists**: Humans remain A**ccountable**

No algorithm should be allowed to become a moral proxy. No system should be treated as neutral simply because it is automated.

Clarity is governance's greatest defence. It must be clear on its roles.

Reframing Progress

Progress does not mean building machines that resemble humans. It means building systems that serve humans and help them flourish.

The question is not:

> ***Can machines think like us?***

The question is:

> ***How can technology help us think better?* And it can ...**

This reframing restores agency. It centres responsibility and places intelligence where it belongs.

The Lie, Finally Exposed

The greatest lie about Ai is not that it will destroy us. It is that even though it has surpassed us in automation, it will never surpass us in intelligence. Ai has not replaced human intelligence because it cannot. It has reflected it, amplified, flattened, and redistributed. What we see in machines is what we put into them.

The danger is not artificial intelligence. It is artificial authority.

A Choice that is Still Ours to Make
We stand at a threshold.
We can:

- Surrender judgment to systems that do not understand
- Or insist that intelligence remains a human obligation

We can:

- Accept fluency as wisdom
- Or demand meaning, ethics, and responsibility

The future will not be predetermined by code. Oh no!

It will be shaped by how honestly, we name what our machines are, and what they are not. There is no shame in what they cannot achieve and no hurry for them to become more.

Artificial Awareness is powerful, just as it is.

Human intelligence is precious, just as it is.

Confusing the two risks losing both.

The machines are not thinking for us, they cannot. The question is whether we will continue to think for ourselves.

CONCLUSION

This book does not argue against Ai. You will find that I support Ai as a tool for creatives and non-creatives alike. This book argues **against the lie that intelligence has already arrived**.

Until machines can understand meaning, bear responsibility, and live with consequences, intelligence remains a human obligation, and a human gift.

The future depends on whether we remember that. Artificial systems can assist us, and extend our reach in ways that were unimaginable only decades ago. To reject that would be both dishonest and unnecessary. We are living in an era where fluency is mistaken for understanding, where speed is confused with wisdom, and where prediction is treated as judgment. Because machines can now speak like us, respond like us, and mirror our reasoning, we are tempted to believe they think like us. But intelligence is not performance. It is not the appearance of competence. It is not the ability to produce convincing answers. Intelligence is the capacity to understand meaning, to form intent, to weigh consequences, and to take responsibility for decisions that affect others.

Until machines can understand meaning, they cannot truly know what they are doing. Until they can bear responsibility, they cannot be trusted with moral authority. Until they can live with consequences, feel them, reflect on them, and be changed by them, they cannot be said to possess intelligence.

What we call Ai today does not meet these conditions. It operates through artificial awareness: powerful, responsive, and increasingly convincing, but ultimately empty of understanding.

This distinction matters because the greatest risk before us is not that machines will become intelligent, but that humans will begin to behave as if they no longer need to be intelligent. When we outsource judgment and/or when we defer responsibility. When we allow systems to decide simply because they can, we do not elevate technology, we diminish ourselves.

Intelligence is not something we should be eager to give away, especially to systems that cannot carry its weight.

Intelligence remains a human obligation because only humans can be accountable. Intelligence remains a human gift because it is rooted in consciousness, inner life, creativity, empathy, and moral imagination. These are qualities no machine currently possesses, no matter how sophisticated it appears.

The future, then, does not hinge on what machines become. It hinges on what humans choose to remember about themselves. We must remember that intelligence is more than output, more than efficiency and more than imitation. We can build a future where Ai serves humanity without replacing its moral centre. But if we forget and mistake artificial awareness for intelligence, we risk surrendering the very qualities that make progress meaningful.

The future depends on whether we remember who we are.

Remember often.

APPENDIX

This appendix exists for one reason: **precision**.

Much of the confusion surrounding Ai does not come from malice or ignorance, but from loose language. When terms are blurred, responsibility is blurred with them. The following sections provide clear definitions and correct common myths.

A. Key Definitions

Agency

The capacity to act independently with intent and responsibility. Ai systems do not possess agency, regardless of how autonomous they appear.

Artificial Awareness

A system's ability to detect inputs, adapt responses, maintain context, and operate dynamically **without understanding, intent, or consciousness**. This is the most accurate description of modern Ai.

Awareness

The ability to detect, process, and respond to stimuli within an environment.

Consciousness

The subjective experience of being, having an inner life, perspective, and sense of existence. No existing Ai system is conscious.

Intelligence

The capacity to understand meaning, form intent, make judgments, revise beliefs, and bear responsibility for consequences.

B. Common Myths vs. Reality

Myth	Reality
Ai thinks	Ai predicts patterns
Ai understands	Ai correlates data
Ai is neutral	Ai reflects human choices
Ai decides	Ai selects based on criteria
Ai creates	Ai recombines
Ai learns like humans	Ai optimizes parameters
Ai is objective	Ai encodes values implicitly

C. Why Anthropomorphic Language Is Dangerous

Phrases like these assign agencies where none exists:

- "The Ai believes"
- "The system decided"
- "The algorithm knows"

These phrases should be replaced with:

- "The system predicted"
- "The model output"
- "The tool recommended"

Language shapes responsibility. Precision preserves it.

D. Questions Policymakers Should Ask Ai Vendors

Before adopting any Ai system, decision-makers should ask:

1. What assumptions are embedded in this system?
2. What data was used, and what was excluded?
3. Who defines success or accuracy?
4. What kinds of errors are acceptable, and to whom?
5. How does the system handle uncertainty?
6. Who is accountable when harm occurs?
7. Can this system explain its outputs meaningfully?
8. What human oversight is required?

If these questions cannot be answered clearly, the system is not ready for use.

E. Ai in Education: A Cautionary Note

Ai can assist learning, but it cannot replace understanding.
Educators should:

- Emphasize critical evaluation of Ai outputs
- Teach students how Ai works conceptually
- Reinforce that fluency does not equal truth

Students must learn to question machines, not defer to them.

F. Ai and Moral Responsibility

No Ai system can:

- Feel guilt
- Experience harm
- Be morally blamed

Responsibility always rests with:

- Designers
- Deployers
- Decision-makers

Any framework that assigns moral agency to machines is avoiding accountability.

G. Final Clarification

Artificial awareness is not a failure of technology. It is a grand achievement.
Naming it accurately:

- Protects human agency
- Preserves accountability
- Enables responsible progress

The goal is not to diminish Ai, but to place it correctly within the human story.

ABOUT THE AUTHOR

Marsha Gomes-Mc Kie is a dynamic force in Caribbean literature, blending storytelling, illustration, and advocacy into a vibrant creative practice. Marsha writes across age groups and genres. She is also an accomplished illustrator, bringing her stories, and those of others to life.

Her entrepreneurial spirit led to the founding of *Aajumbee Publishing House*, an independent press dedicated to amplifying Caribbean voices and mythologies. Through this venture, Marsha publishes her own work and supports fellow creatives in bringing their stories to market.

Even though Ai has threatened to overtake Marsha's creative life, she has embraced it fully on her entrepreneurial journey. This partnership allows her to draw a clear line between books created for profit and books crafted from the soul. Having overcome the fear of taking the plunge, Marsha now speaks with authority and empathy to other creatives navigating the evolving landscape of Ai. She has grown her business while maintaining her creative edge.

Beyond publishing, Marsha is a passionate literary advocate. She founded the *Caribbean Books Foundation*, a platform that connects authors across the region, launched Caribbean Folklore Month in 2022 and celebrates Caribbean literature. She also serves as Regional Advisor for the Caribbean South's Chapter of the Society of Children's Book Writers and Illustrators (SCBWI).

Marsha's journey is one of innovation, and cultural pride. Her work bridges generations and geographies, leaving a lasting imprint on readers and creators alike.

Registered with the Artist Registry of the Ministry of Culture of Trinidad and Tobago.

📧 Contact: mgomesmckie@gmail.com
📚 Find her on: Amazon | Goodreads

OTHER BOOKS

This book is for writers, illustrators, educators, and indie/self-publishers, with a strong emphasis on indigenous creators. As we navigate the void of Ai, we must always come out stronger, and this is how you do it.

I generally have one question I ask myself in the use of Ai – does using Ai in this instance, diminish or increase my creative skillset? Is my creative skillset being eroded or maintained. A simple example, if you are a romance author, you must protect that skillset by continuing to write romance. Ai can be used to assist you in research, mapping characters, proofreading, social media and marketing visuals and text; however, the value of your creative input must not be handed over to Ai. It must always be a collaboration.

At a conference recently, I was asked the question, can an author be an author in the age of Ai? The answer is a resounding, yes. An author is a creator of words and worlds and even though we have entered a new phase of technology that gives authors new options to complete the task of writing, the author's style of writing remains the same.

I maintain that artificial intelligence will not surpass the ingenuity of the human creative mind, as creativity cannot be precisely duplicated or fully mapped for replication. The most innovative thinkers are often characterized by their unpredictability, a quality that Ai cannot be trained to emulate. While some may perceive this stance as sentimental, my perspective is also grounded in practical considerations. Ai's commercial value is contingent on its role as a support tool that can be monetized by individuals or organizations. The simple truth is that if Ai becomes too efficient, enough to replace the user, it will lose its monetary value.

In the contemporary economic landscape, the integration of artificial intelligence raises questions regarding compensation for its developers. Ideally, Ai should evolve into an indispensable companion for users, generating revenue through monthly subscription models. It is unlikely that business owners would eliminate their subscriber base in favour of performing creative tasks independently without being paid.

Even if Ai reaches that plateau where it can work independently of humans; the question still remains how do you make money from Ai when it has undermined the payment model? And the payment model is based on you, the creative paying for Ai as a companion service. The economics of Ai doing anything else will be its downfall, meaning any independently aware Ai will become a threat to capitalism and will be taken offline in favour of a companion model.

Ai will reach its threshold for profit and will remain right in that zone and those who wish to push Ai further will meet opposition.

Ai is new but it is here to stay and will do things that will blow our minds. Human ingenuity came before it and will outlast it, simply because human ingenuity wants to make a profit on it.

Do not be concerned with becoming obsolete, we must not fear or alienate Ai, the time is now to learn from and partner with it. As artificial intelligence continues to evolve, it is essential for us to guide its development responsibly. Progress in Ai is inevitable, so it is important to remain confident in our ability to innovate and excel, both with and without the support of emerging technologies.

As a writer, illustrator, photographer and visual artist, Ai has hit me on all fronts. Every creative endeavour now has an upgrade, yet in the last year my income has increased. I didn't throw my hands up and say well let me find a new profession(s). I learned Ai and am able to market my services, with or without it. I have clients who wish for me to use Ai, and I can, and then I have those who don't want any Ai, and I can provide that as well. The world will remain with these two partitions Before-Ai (BA) and After-Ai (AA), and I can survive on both islands.

From an individual perspective, there were questions about maintaining originality when incorporating Ai. I am pleased to say the integration of Ai has not disrupted my creative workflow. I view Ai as one of several tools at my disposal - comparable to choosing between walking, driving, taking a bus, or flying - for achieving objectives efficiently and cost-effectively. I maintain a strong commitment to my original creative projects, which are personally meaningful and undertaken independently.

These endeavours typically require three to six months to complete. As an independent publisher, I now balance the development of original works with the production of more generic titles to expand market reach. This dual approach enables me to manage two distinct creative processes and effectively double the number of books produced within the same timeframe.

This morning, I created my own drawing in Procreate for an original children's book, and in the afternoon, I am continuing work on this book, where charts and pictures will be generated by Ai. Everything in life has both advantages and disadvantages, and it is the individual's responsibility to determine them.

Ai and the Creative Entrepreneur will give you clear rules-of-engagement and a framework with ready-to-use templates, prompts, checklists, and workflows for making books and growing a creative business with Ai - ethically and sustainably.

Stay safe,
Marsha Gomes-Mc Kie

Made in the USA
Monee, IL
03 November 2026

67386721R00049